JONAH
AND
A VERY BIG FISH
by Sunny Griffin

Illustrated by Yacoba

DID YOU KNOW... God told Jonah to go into a city called Nineveh and tell everyone about Him?

DID YOU KNOW...
Jonah didn't want
to go because he was
afraid of the wicked
people in Nineveh?

DID YOU KNOW...
When Jonah got on
a ship and went out
on the sea,
he was trying to
hide from God?

DID YOU KNOW...
God knew Jonah
was on the ship
and he sent a terrible
storm to make
him come back?

DID YOU KNOW...
The wind blew
so hard that the
sailors were afraid
the ship would sink
and they would
all die?

DID YOU KNOW...
Jonah knew God had sent the terrible storm because he had not obeyed Him?

DID YOU KNOW...

When Jonah told the sailors to throw him into the sea and God would stop the storm, they did?

DID YOU KNOW...
God sent a very big fish up out of the water to save Jonah from drowning?

DID YOU KNOW...
After the very big
fish opened his
mouth real wide and
swallowed Jonah, he
went back down
into the sea?

DID YOU KNOW...

Jonah thanked God for saving him while he was down in the dark, smelly belly of the very big fish?

DID YOU KNOW...
It was three days before the very big fish brought Jonah up to the seashore and let him go?

DID YOU KNOW...

Jonah knew he never wanted to run away from God again and he happily obeyed Him?

Jonah went to Nineveh and told the people about God. They listened and gave up their wicked ways.